STERLING INNOVATION
New York

An Imprint of Sterling Publishing
1166 Avenue of the Americas
New York, NY 10036

ISBN 978-1-4351-6149-8

This book is part of *Zen Garden* and is not to be sold separately.

For information about custom editions, special sales, and premium and corporate
purchases, please contact Sterling Special Sales at 800-805-5489
or specialsales@sterlingpublishing.com.

Manufactured in China.

www.sterlingpublishing.com

1 3 5 7 9 10 8 6 4 2 0

zen garden

Written by David Holzer

STERLING INNOVATION
New York

Ah, how glorious!
Green leaves, young leaves
Glittering in the sunlight.

Matsuo Basho (1644–1694)
Japanese poet

Contents

Introduction

Sen-no-Rikyu, a sixteenth century tea master, built a garden enclosed by a tall hedge that blocked the view of the sea. The client for whom the garden was built was unhappy—until he bent to wash his hands in the water basin.

From this position the sea became visible in a gap between the hedges, and the client smiled.

As the tea master had hoped, the client realized the intent behind the design. His mind made the connection between the water in the basin and the great ocean, and thus between himself and the infinite universe.

"The perfection of Zen is to be perfectly and simply human."

Alan Watts (1915–1973)
English scholar and writer

The world of Zen gardens is both fascinating and beautiful. This book provides an introduction to how, and why, Zen gardens developed and why they are so popular all over the world.

In recent years, more and more Western people from all walks of life have become interested in the teachings of Buddhism. Buddhism offers a way of interpreting the nature of our existence and learning to deal with the stresses of modern life. A major part of the way in which followers of Zen Buddhism try to arrive at an understanding of life and beyond is through contemplation and meditation, which require serene environments such as Zen gardens.

Zen gardens were usually found in the grounds of Zen temples, hence their name. They weren't necessarily created using Zen principles, but monks and other followers of Zen found them peaceful, restful places in which to practice their religious reveries.

Today, Zen gardens can be found anywhere in the world, and not just for their contemplative properties. They also appeal to gardeners because they are reasonably easy to build. The dryness of the frequently used sand and rock also reduces the need for maintenance.

Depending on how complicated the landscape is, it's also possible to experiment with creating different kinds of Zen gardens. There are a number of design principles that can be used when making your own garden, and you can read more about these later.

Zen gardens can also disarm Western viewers, causing them to look at the world in a different light. This is simply because Zen gardens are so different from the gardens we experience every day.

Charming miniature Zen gardens are also available and many can retain the design principles and methods of the real gardens. Placed somewhere in your home or office, they can be a reminder of the pleasures of sitting quietly in a Zen garden on a beautiful day.

What is Zen Buddhism?

To come to grips with Zen it helps to have a basic understanding of Buddhism, the religion, or philosophy, of which it is a part.

Buddhism begins with the teachings of Siddhartha Gautama. He was a prince in what is now India in around 500 BC and was raised to a life of supreme comfort. Part of this meant not being exposed to suffering in any form.

At the age of twenty-nine however, Siddhartha was exposed to misery. Some Buddhists

When you are ready to learn a teacher will appear.

believe that this took place in the course of a single chariot ride where he saw an old man, a sick man, a corpse, and a monk.

Deeply troubled, Siddhartha understood that he was to become a monk. He turned his back on his life of privilege and decided to search for understanding.

At the age of thirty-five, Siddhartha achieved enlightenment and became known as the Buddha, which roughly means "one who is awake."

This enlightenment led him to realize that everything in existence changes. Clinging to circumstances and things that are bound to change because of their very nature causes suffering and unhappiness.

If you recognize that constant change is the nature of existence and there is no point in becoming attached to anything, including yourself or the idea of "I," you stop suffering.

One of the most remarkable things about Buddhism is the way in which it continues to be relevant and applicable to all areas of life, including the sciences. Once you get into the world of atoms and sub-atomic particles it becomes apparent that everything is actually in a constant state of change.

The Birth of Zen

All forms of Buddhism are passed down from teacher to student. In around AD 475, a Buddhist teacher called Bodhidharma traveled from India to China and began to teach the way of Buddhism.

Once in China, Buddhism began to take on elements of Taoism. At that time, Taoism was the native Chinese religion. The outcome of this mixture of the two religions, or philosophies, was the Ch'an School of Buddhism.

When you reach the top keep climbing.

Around AD 1200, Ch'an Buddhism spread from China to Japan. In Japan it became known as Zen, a loose translation of Ch'an.

The aim of all Zen Buddhists is to reach "satori," the state the Buddha reached when he meditated under the bodhi tree and became enlightened.

Zen and words

The answers to the historical questions "how did Zen come to exist?" and "what is the essence of Zen?" are very different.

In Zen literature across the centuries, the question "what is the essence of Zen?" has been asked in a number of different ways. These include: "what is the meaning of Bodhidharma coming from the West?" or even the more abstract question of "have you eaten yet?".

Only the individual can answer these questions. The answers cannot be based on something you have taken from a book or what a teacher has told you.

Zen teachers would suggest that the best answer is "practice." The point is that, according to Zen Buddhists, truth or meaning have an existence beyond words. They may or may not contain truth.

We need to realize that the nature of existence is beyond anything we can describe in words. In everyday life, words are simply a convenient tool.

Types of Zen Garden

The styles of Zen garden are varied and steeped in meanings that are open to continual interpretation.

Dry rock gardens

Dry rock gardens aim to inspire the same calm induced through the contemplation of pure nature but in a highly stylized way. Waters are represented with sand or pebbles, mountains with stone, and islands with masses of moss or rock.

From the withered tree a flower blooms.

Although the garden at Ryoan-ji is probably the most famous example of a dry rock garden in Japan, the garden at Tenryu-ji is also an interesting example.

Tenryu-ji was the first of the five great Zen temples to be built in Kyoto. A famous garden designer named Muso Soseki transformed the existing garden at the temple into a Zen masterpiece by adding seven vertical rocks.

It is argued that this arrangement of rocks refers to a Zen fable about a fish that had the strength and power to swim up a waterfall. Once at the top of the waterfall, the fish transformed itself into a dragon.

Similarly, the arrangements of rocks at the foot of a waterfall in a Japanese garden, dry or otherwise, are thought to be symbolic of carp.

Carp are highly regarded and prized in both Chinese and Japanese culture for their strength, cunning, and spirit.

Whatever the identity of the fish, the principle behind the arrangement may well be the same. The rocks, like the fable, are meant to inspire the inner strength and discipline that is central to becoming a Zen master.

With dry rock pools, the sand is raked regularly in a certain pattern, the arrangement of which relates to the symbolism of the garden. Rake lines might suggest currents around rocks, for instance, while the act of raking itself is something that helps the Zen practitioner in contemplation.

It is good to have an end to journey toward, but it is the journey that matters in the end.

Stroll gardens

The Zen Buddhist appreciation of juxtaposition means that dry rock gardens are often found near lush, green gardens. Unlike the dry rock gardens, sometimes meant to be contemplated from inside a house, stroll or strolling gardens are places to walk in and reflect upon the nature of existence.

A good example of this kind of juxtaposition is at the Koke-dera, or Moss Temple, at the Saiho-ji Temple in Kyoto.

Here, the design of the garden has been enhanced by an abundance of moss that has accumulated over the years. The fact this has been allowed to happen is in stark contrast to the control exercised over dry rock gardens. With dry rock examples, every effort is made to keep the garden and its design as close as possible to what was intended.

It could be suggested that nature being allowed to alter the garden designer's conception adds to the purpose for which stroll gardens were created.

Stroll gardens originated in India where walking around a temple is symbolic of strolling around the spiritual center of the universe. When Buddhism traveled from India to China, the concept of the stroll garden was adapted.

The Chinese decorated their gardens with symbols of the Buddhist universe. Every time a stroller encountered a symbol it helped purify his or her mind.

With the development of Zen, stroll gardens evolved still further. A stroll garden of the kind seen at Koke Dera tries to create the illusion of a long journey within a limited amount of space. A twisting path, which here wraps around a pond, has objects or symbols placed at the bends to keep the stroller's mind on the spiritual.

Stroll gardens are also ideal places for Zen Buddhists to practice walking meditation, or "kinhin."

Strolling pond gardens

A variation on the stroll garden is the strolling pond garden, or "chisen kaiyo shiki." This type of garden is made up of two ponds that are often connected by a large wooden bridge arching over the upper pond.

The style of this bridge will often be influenced by Chinese half-moon bridges, sufficiently arched for boats to pass underneath.

In Japanese ponds, stones are often symbolically submerged. The most common symbolism is a representation of the islands of the paradise of Amida Buddhism.

With strolling pond gardens, two large stones are submerged in the lower pond. These represent a tortoise and a crane, symbolizing long life and good health.

14

Tea gardens

Tea gardens, or "rojiniwa," feature the elements that have become popular in Western versions of Japanese garden design.

In a tea garden, stone lanterns, stepping stones, and the traditional stone water basin are carefully arranged according to their symbolic meaning—but the most important element of a rojiniwa is the ceremonial teahouse where the famous Japanese tea ceremony is performed.

Natural gardens

Natural gardens, called "shukeiyen" in Japanese, are often made up of intricately designed waterfalls and a pond.

They can be viewed from under the shelter of a gazebo, or "azumaya." In line with Japanese geomantic principles of garden design—which are very similar to feng shui—the view of the garden from the azumaya is carefully considered. Features and elements of the design are carefully placed according to both aesthetic and philosophical principles. Natural gardens will usually have a pavilion and a gatehouse as well.

The Principles of Zen Garden Design

Apart from their beauty and the effect they create, the way in which Japanese Zen gardens are designed is fascinating. Traditional Western gardens are more concerned with the display of trees, shrubs, plants, and flowers almost for their own sake. In Zen gardens, the placement of every item serves a purpose.

Sitting quietly, doing nothing, springs come and grass grows by itself.

Change and design

Before exploring the principles of Japanese Zen garden design, it's important to remember that the intentions of the original designer(s) can never be known for certain.

Plants and trees also grow and die, water levels rise and fall, and rocks can be added, subtracted, or repositioned. Many of the most famous Japanese gardens have been changed, often considerably, over time.

Wherever it is in the world, a garden is nearly always a work in progress. At the same time, nature has a way of changing even the most considered and well-preserved design.

With so many variable factors, the following sections discuss the general design principles, rather than the minute details of specific gardens.

It's also necessary to be aware of the fact that, just because gardens are found in Zen temples, they haven't automatically been designed according to Zen principles.

Zen and design principles

Many people who study Japanese gardens give various elements meanings that relate specifically to Zen or Buddhism in general. A good example is the three rocks found in ponds which are nearly always taken to represent the paradise of Amida Buddhism. Although this may well be true, absolute proof that this was the designer's intention is, more often than not, hard to find.

Certain elements of Japanese gardens come from Shinto—the use of trees and stones, for instance. Shinto means "the way of the gods" and it was a religion that believed gods lived everywhere in the natural world. The gardens should really be seen as beautiful, slightly mysterious expressions of the whole of Japanese thought and culture.

Geomancy
in Brief

Geomancy, or what became known as feng shui in the nineteenth century, plays an important part in Japanese garden design. Like so much in Japanese culture, geomancy was brought from China to Japan.

Originally, geomancy was an ancient form of divination. A seer would scatter handfuls of soil on the ground or create markings in earth or sand and then "read" them.

Entering the forest, the enlightened man does not disturb a blade of grass.

This developed into a system of determining the location and orientation of houses, tombs, and other buildings. In feng shui, which means wind and water, the belief is that there are powerful currents and lines of magnetism that run over the landscape and surface of the earth.

The landscape will display both yin (negative) and yang (positive) features. Gently undulating country is yin, or female. Sharp rocks and steep mountains are yang, or male.

Feng shui masters locate sites where the energies of the land, or its "ch'i," and sky are brought into perfect balance. This harmony means good fortune.

They will also locate structures in positions that influence the way in which the landscape is viewed. In Japanese garden design, this principle sits alongside the way in which gardens are created so that certain features can be seen in a specific way.

For instance, some gardens are meant to be contemplated from a certain angle— perhaps the viewer will be seated inside a temple or house.

At the same time, every feature of a landscape can be altered, or created to produce harmony. According to feng shui masters, when a landscape is beautiful it is because the lines of the magnetic currents girdling the planet earth are in balance.

A Brief History of Zen Gardens

The beautiful Zen gardens that are so admired today are the product of the evolution of garden design throughout Japanese history.

Zen gardens were also influenced by dramatic changes taking place in Japanese life, religion, and culture. These shifts in circumstances inspired designers to create new gardens and traditions.

There are six main periods of Japanese garden design which conform to consistent principles. It's important to remember that the interpretation placed on a garden might not have been what the designer meant.

The god spirit garden

Two of the elements in garden design, as it was imported from Korea and China in the sixth century AD, already existed in Japan for religious reasons—stones and ponds.

Still employed in Japanese garden design today, stones and ponds were used in Shinto, the ancient religion of Japan.

Certain divine spirits could be found in particular places like islands, ancient trees, stones, and ponds. This connection between Buddhist principles of garden design and Shinto beliefs seems highly likely to have helped the development of Zen gardens.

Poetry and Paradise in Harmony

To the mind
that is still
the whole
universe
surrenders.

Between 794 and 1185 (also known as
the Heian period of Japanese history),
gardens began to be built in the town
houses of the aristocracy. These gardens
used images relating to paradise, as
well as poetic images and the principles
of geomancy.

Paradise—in the form of the Pure Land, a Buddhist heaven—was shown by a group of three islands. These were surrounded by a pond that represented the ocean that separates unenlightened mortals from reaching heaven. Designers also used an arched bridge connecting the island to the shore, to suggest the potential of salvation.

In gardens of this period it is possible to see the application of geomancy principles in the positioning of specific plants or rocks in relation to the flow of water in a garden to create harmony—balancing yin (the negative, passive force) and yang (the positive, active force) and the five elements of wood, fire, earth, metal, and water.

As with religion, the poetry of the period was full of images of the Japanese natural world. These were used as a way to express the poet's own feelings. It's logical to assume that the same images were used in the creation of gardens for similar reasons.

The gardens themselves then become collections of poetic images, mixed in with ideas of Buddhist paradise and Japanese principles of harmonious design.

means "dry-mountain-water." So, the garden was an image of mountains and water, created without using water itself.

Inspiration for the gardens came from the very simple black and white ink paintings from the Southern Sung dynasty in China. These paintings reduced a landscape to a few highly controlled brushstrokes.

Garden designers used these principles to create gardens using only specific evergreen plants, rocks, sand, or moss, which were enclosed by a wall or hedge.

Dry-mountain-water gardens

In the Muromachi period, between 1333 and 1573, the warrior class took control of Japanese society. At this time, a new form of garden style developed in the Zen Buddhist temples and warrior houses.

A highly stylized garden was built into a small courtyard next to a sitting room. The name of this kind of garden is "karesansui," which

The idea was that you didn't physically enter the garden, but looked at it from your seat in the nearby room or from a veranda. In this way, the garden became something to contemplate, as you would a painting or sculpture.

Emptiness, and what was left out of the garden design, became very important and kept in line with both Zen Buddhist principles and the art of the Muromachi period.

Entering the teahouse

The tea ceremony called "wabi-cha," developed in the Momoyama period between 1574 and 1600 and resulted in the development of a new form of garden called "roji."

Wabi-cha came about as a rebellion against the ostentatiousness of the then rulers of Japan. Its creators championed the beauty in things that had imperfections or were old. This simple beauty could be found in rustic life, particularly in the crude bowls in which tea was served in the wabi-cha ceremony.

Although not actually gardens, the purpose of the roji was to prepare a person who was taking part in the tea ceremony. These spaces provided a passage that the participant in a tea ceremony would walk through, preparing themselves spiritually and physically to enter the teahouse.

When someone walked through a roji garden, across a series of thresholds that were barely noticeable, the aim was to forget the world, clearing the mind and allowing full appreciation and concentration during the wabi-cha.

Tsubo gardens

Between 1600 and 1868, the Edo period, urban Japanese merchants began to dominate culture.

To avoid the taxes charged on the width of a building's facade, merchants developed a long, narrow type of architecture that combined a shop and residence. The shop was at the front of the building, with space for one or two family areas toward the back. Small spaces for light and air were left open between these homes.

When the owners of these properties became wealthier, they began to commission gardens to be built in the spaces, which were often minute. The designs of these gardens incorporated elements from tea gardens, partly because of necessity and also because the owners were merchants and not ostentatious aristocrats.

The small size and enclosed nature of these private gardens gave rise to their name, "tsubo"—the size of two tatami mats being called a tsubo.

The Elements of Zen Gardens

Bridges (Hashi)

Bridges have profound symbolic meanings in most cultures and the same is true of Japanese philosophy. Here, bridges are believed to enable the transition from one world to another—a link between the different stages in human life.

The bridge is an integral part of Japanese garden design. Gardens that included ponds would nearly always include bridges that connected islands with each other and the shore.

The ponds and islands came to symbolize the Amida Buddhist paradise and bridges connecting islands to the shore suggested the journey between this world and the next one. And as far as Zen specifically is concerned, they can suggest the journey toward enlightenment.

In the Heian period in particular, bridges on the larger boating ponds would be built of wood or stone and arched to allow boats to pass beneath them. These bridges, inspired by the Chinese "full moon bridge" have nearly all disappeared.

Later on, when gardens often had ponds that were too small for boats, bridges could be made of simple natural, uncut slabs of stone with between one and three slabs being used.

Bridges can also be found in the "kare-san-sui," or dry landscape gardens, where their purpose is purely symbolic as they cross a stream made from sand or gravel.

Apart from the rough slab bridges, Japanese gardens could contain simple wooden bridges, which were made of logs laid parallel to each other and supported on a frame. Sometimes far more elaborate, covered bridges were built that looked almost like pavilions.

Flowers (Hana)

Typical Western gardens are characterized by many flowering plants. This is not so true of Japanese gardens, particularly those connected to Zen gardens. This is probably due to the emphasis upon the symbolic meaning for each carefully selected item and the role of these items as a source for meditation.

However, Japanese gardens have not always been devoid of flowering plants. During the Heian period an enormous variety of flowering plants, trees, vines, reeds, and grasses were very common. This could have something to do with the role played by gardens in this period as a means of displaying the wealth of their owners.

As Japanese gardens evolved, flowering plants came to be used less and less, although they can still be found in the historic gardens of Japan. Water-loving plants, like the iris, water lily, and lotus, are often found.

Irises have been used for their medicinal properties for centuries in Japan and they also have a symbolic meaning. Lotuses are extremely important in Buddhism as they symbolize enlightenment—roots embedded in the mud of human passions and flowers open to sunlight and purity.

Apart from flowering plants, shrubs and vines, such as hydrangea and wisteria, are used in both medieval and modern gardens. Azaleas and rhododendrons contribute color and are often pruned and shaped to represent the rolling hills found in Yamato-e landscape paintings.

31

Sand (Suna)

When most people think of Japanese gardens they think of raked sand. "Shirakawasuna," or white raked sand, is particularly characteristic.

The origins of this might lie in the history of Shinto, the religion native to Japan. Historians believe that the earliest Shinto shrines might have been forest clearings. To purify the ground and make it acceptable to the spirits of Shinto, a layer of washed sand or gravel was laid down.

This argument is borne out by the historical Shinto shrines that still exist where, in between the various structures, there is often a simple rectangle of white sand.

Areas of white sand are also associated with the Japanese royal family, who are believed to be of divine ancestry. Visitors to the Imperial Palace in Kyoto will have witnessed this association and noted the broad expanse of white sand in front of the palace.

Apart from these sacred associations, sand was also used by designers in later periods to draw upon. In these instances, areas of sand came to symbolize oceans or rivers and were raked to suggest currents or waves.

Perhaps the clearest example of this is the corner garden at Daisen-in in Kyoto. Here raked sand is meant to represent a stream flowing from the mountains.

In some cases, though, it's more difficult to prove that the patterns of raking were suggestive of anything. In Ryoan-ji, for instance, the idea that sand equals water is not so easy to prove.

Stones (Ishi/Iwakura)

Stones, whether large or small, feature prominently—in every sense—in most Japanese gardens and have done so since the very start of garden design. Indeed, the opening line of the Sakuteiki talks about the setting of stones.

The use of stones and the reverence with which they are regarded have their roots in Shinto, as with so much of Japanese garden design.

Experts in Japanese garden design also argue that the placing of stones, or groups of stones, is also intended to be symbolic of mountain ranges sacred to Hindu, Buddhist, and Taoist mythology.

According to this train of thought, groups of three stones, called "sanzonseki," were intended to invoke the Buddhist trinity, or sanzonbutsu. The problem lies in the fact that there is no direct evidence in the form of writings by contemporary garden designers to confirm that this is the case.

Certain stones were almost certainly intended to represent mountains though and early Japanese and Chinese texts make this quite clear.

The range of actual stones used by garden designers is remarkably varied in terms of shapes, textures, and colors. Daisen-in dry garden is a good example of this. Here there is a wide range of shapes and surfaces among the rocks that have been used.

As with all elements in garden design, rocks also have symbolic significance. Writings on Japanese gardens give detailed lists of rock shapes with natural and Buddhist meanings. These include "tiger's head stone," "Buddha's footprint," and "sleeping buffalo."

The most common shape, though, is a tall, mountain-shaped stone that often forms a centerpiece, called "omo ishi." This is placed with a group of smaller stones and a low, flat stone.

Arranging stones in this way follows the principle established by theorists of Chinese landscape painting. The rock island of Tenryu-ji garden is a good example of this principle at work.

Trees (Ki)

The most commonly appearing trees in Japanese gardens are pines, maples, bamboo, camellias, cherries, and flowering plums.

In the Heian period, more unusual trees, such as orange trees and oaks, might have been seen. As with flowering shrubs, which were also more prominent in this era, this is possibly due to the role the garden played in displaying its owner's wealth.

Trees are as sacred as stones in Japan's Shinto religion, which believed that god spirits lived in all natural things. This is why trees have always been important as symbols in Japanese garden design. It's important to remember, though, that ancient gardens would not necessarily have been as heavily wooded as they've been allowed to become today.

The pine, bamboo, and flowering plum are considered the "Three Friends of Winter" in Japan and China. Both the bamboo and pine keep their leaves and needles throughout winter and the plum blossoms even before the snow has melted.

These properties have led to the trees representing human character and endurance in the face of adversity. Pines, especially, are a metaphor for aged individuals who've weathered the tests of time. This is why Japanese gardeners traditionally trained evergreens in the image of ancient pines.

The brief flowering of the cherry and plum trees is intended to symbolize the fragile nature of both natural beauty and life itself, as does the turning and falling of maple leaves.

Cherry and plum trees also add color to Japanese gardens. To the designer however, the fact that the color passes is what is most significant. It adds to the general feeling of melancholy which characterizes much Japanese art and, in turn, Zen gardens.

Plants Typically Found in Zen Gardens

Be a spot on the ground where nothing is growing, where something might be planted, a seed, from the absolute.

Trees, shrubs and plants are always planted with great care in Japanese gardens. While some plants have symbolic meanings, all form part of the overall design.

When creating your garden, it is wise to exert a similar amount of care and planning to create a Zen garden you can enjoy and be proud of.

Take into account obvious factors such as the dimensions of your garden, light patterns, and soil type. Not all your plants need be traditional choices, but should you wish to include authentic varieties the following trees, shrubs, and plants are typically found in Zen gardens.

Large, background evergreen trees

Evergreen trees are used to frame the design of the garden and provide background for specific features.

The camphor tree is an exotic, aromatic tree that is widely used for ornamental purposes. It grows between 45 and 90 feet high and can be as broad as it is tall. Densely covered with shiny leaves, camphor is an excellent background tree. In spring, it grows three-inch spikes of very small yellowish-white flowers.

The Japanese umbrella pine, which grows to form a pyramid shape, is also widely used. On young trees, the branches stick straight out, but over time come to look like the ribs on an umbrella. The orange, peeling bark of the tree is ornamental but is usually hidden. Other popular trees include the cedar, holly oak, and Japanese black pine.

Large, deciduous trees

These are used to give a focus in garden design and include the black locust, which has beautiful, fragrant flowers that bloom three to four weeks after the start of spring growth. Black locust trees usually have a vertical oval shape.

The maidenhair tree, also known as gingko, is popular with gardeners, but it can grow up to 75 feet tall by 60 feet wide. This means that it is best suited to large gardens. As it ages, the maidenhair tree forms a majestic, massive pyramid. Other popular deciduous trees are the Chinese pistachio, green ebony, sweet gum, and tulip trees.

Medium-sized evergreen trees

Trees of this kind are used as border trees. The beautiful evergreen dogwood is popular because it is long flowering, with smallish greeny-yellow flowers that mature into a cream yellow and fade to a faint pink. After flowering, fleshy crimson red, strawberry-shaped fruit appear.

The loquat—also called May apple, Japanese medlar, or Japanese plum—is highly prized for its large, rich evergreen foliage and tasty edible fruit. This is considered a great delicacy in the Orient.

Other popular trees are the golden mimosa, holly, and magnolia.

> Many paths lead from
> The foot of the mountain,
> But at the peak
> We all gaze at the
> single bright moon

Ikkyu (1394–1481)

Medium-sized deciduous trees

You can use trees of this kind to provide contrast. The golden-chain tree provides a brightly colored focus in spring with its glorious yellow flowers.

Other particularly striking trees are the Japanese pagoda tree, which can grow to be 60 feet tall and wide, and the katsura tree. This has heart-shaped leaves which are blue-green in the summer, turning scarlet to yellow in the fall. Katsura trees often have more than one trunk.

Small deciduous trees

These trees can be used for framing features and providing contrast when they blossom.

The Japanese lilac tree is a deciduous shrub that can grow to 24 feet high and 18 feet wide. It is a popular ornamental plant because it produces white flowers in early summer.

The smoke tree is also popular for its clusters of long, thin, hair-like flowers which appear in early May. From June to September, the smoke tree produces small, egg-shaped, fleshy fruit.

Gardeners also choose the Japanese maple, Brazilian butterfly tree, and showy crab apple trees.

Creating your own Japanese Garden

Although it's rooted in centuries of history, Japanese garden design is a living tradition and one which you can become part of by creating your own garden.

In the West, some of the designs and principles used in Japanese gardens have more, not less, relevance today. With smaller amounts of space available, the significance of how a garden can be viewed to make it seem larger becomes more important.

Do your work, then step back. The only path to serenity.

42

Techniques of miniaturization, balancing composition and harmony as well as using rock and water features, are also increasingly relevant.

Another reason for increased interest in the West might lie in the way in which Japanese designers aimed to arrive at the essence of nature in their designs. In the West, more and more people live in cities and towns. They are removed from nature and, therefore, seek out ways to bring themselves closer to the natural world.

Again, Japanese and Chinese gardens concentrate on showing man in harmony with nature. Nature is not controlled and organized. The aim with Japanese gardens is to feel at ease with nature, partly because of the belief that god spirits dwell everywhere in nature, especially in rocks and stones.

If you're interested in creating gardens within the tradition of Japanese garden design, it's not really a question of littering your garden with the trappings. Ornaments such as stone lanterns don't automatically create a Zen garden.

Your aim should be to try to engage with the tradition and use the principles to express your own personal beliefs, tastes, and circumstances.

Another thing to bear in mind is that the design principles and suggested elements outlined in the following pages can be adapted to gardens of just about any size. Japanese gardens have never been simply one size only.

Design Principles

Certain design principles are consistent in Japanese gardens and can be applied to your own garden design.

Enclosure

Principles of enclosure are used in all Japanese gardens for a number of reasons. Enclosure makes a garden into a private space that can be quiet and calm. The city is separated from the garden.

Devices used to enclose a garden—a bamboo fence, perhaps—can also act as a backdrop to the other elements used in its design.

Take up a blade of grass and use it as a golden Buddha, 16 feet high.

Anything you use to enclose a garden should ideally be neutral so that it complements, or at least doesn't interfere with, your composition. The Japanese choose fences and screens that are made from natural, rustic materials.

As well as providing a backdrop, the enclosing device can also screen out anything that potentially spoils the effect of your design. You might want to place a screen in front of a neighbor's fence. If you do so, it's important that the screen is not see-through.

You can also place single screens between elements you have used in your design, like a water basin or arrangement of plants. In this way, you can highlight the feature and block out what is behind it.

The natural elements are also commonly used for enclosure. The sky is important, but your design shouldn't incorporate too much as it creates an imbalance of yang, or positive energy, according to Japanese philosophy.

Viewpoints

The direction in which compositions are meant to be viewed is very important in Japanese garden design. Unlike Western gardens, Japanese gardens, unless they're stroll gardens, are not usually designed for people to wander through.

When you're designing your garden, you need to establish the viewpoint you want to start from. You also need to decide if the garden is to be appreciated from a sitting or standing position.

45

No snowflake ever falls in the wrong place.

Recreating the harmony and balance in nature is a key part of Japanese gardens. To get this right, designers spend time studying nature in the raw and looking at paintings and sculpture to see how artists view natural phenomena.

Harmony and Composition

Examination of the natural world brings about an understanding of how nature works and enables designers to absorb its essence. For instance, you could look at the way a stream winds its way through a landscape.

It was through looking closely at natural landscapes from an artistic perspective that Japanese designers realized that capturing the essence of nature was all about simplification and refinement. Symbolism in a garden composition could speak volumes—a rock could become a mountain and an area of raked gravel a sea.

Studying nature intently led to the discovery that balance was not achieved through symmetry; a sense of harmony was more likely to be achieved in an asymmetrical arrangement. This is why the elements in a design are always grouped in odd numbers.

At the same time, designers learned how to use space and scale, making sure that elements didn't appear out of scale with their neighbors or anything else in the garden.

This principle can be applied to any design, for example, checking that things such as stone lanterns aren't the wrong scale for your garden. If they are, partially screen them with a plant or a strategically placed mound of earth or rock.

Change and contrast

In Japanese garden design, contrast between elements is used to create an impact. The contrast is not simply between elements, but also color and texture.

Designers may use a number of evergreen shrubs to give continuity, and contrast them with a deciduous open-branched shrub or tree—a composition creating its greatest impact in the fall.

Carefully positioned ornaments create a sense of change and expectancy and surprise can be achieved by using gateways, screens, and fences with gaps for people to walk through.

Design Elements

The way in which the design elements in Japanese gardens are used is unique to Japan.

If you try to aim for it, you are running away from it.

Rocks

As we've seen, rocks are very important in Japanese garden design for both religious and aesthetic reasons. This is why they're always placed in a garden before any planting is done.

The most popular rocks in Japanese garden design are old and weathered, ideally with growths of lichen and moss. Round or square rocks, as well as dressed or cut stone, are not used.

Color and texture are also very important, with the Japanese preferring subdued colors. In some cases, though, stones with striking colors might be used for contrast in the right place.

We don't have as much choice of stone in the West, but you should be able to find something suitable in your local nursery. Look for durable, reasonably angular rock—granite, limestone, or sandstone—which is as wide as it is long. If possible, try to find rock that looks weathered.

It's also important to try to see as many faces of the rock as possible. Study rocks in nature and in other Japanese gardens to see how they sit in the ground.

You need to sink rocks into the ground by at least one third of their height to make them stable and so they look natural. Bear this in mind when you're deciding which should be the top and front face of the rock.

When you're buying rocks, you need to remember the perspective of your garden. Think also about the theme of your composition. Rugged, angular rocks are great for suggesting mountains but not for a waterside.

Placing rocks

A rock will look balanced if its outline seems to be heading away from its center of gravity where it meets the ground. If rocks have any strata or veining, make sure it looks as natural as possible and all flows in the same direction. Avoid artificial-looking, fiberglass rocks.

50

Water

Using water in your garden design will give it constant motion and also the extra appeal of pleasant trickling, gurgling sounds. If you're working with a decent-sized body of water it will also release negative ions that help give a sense of health and well-being.

Pond design

Wherever the Japanese use water, it only moves in a way that is natural. For instance, it can be a pond, stream, or waterfall but never a fountain. However it's used, water is always kept crystal clear and moving to symbolize purity.

If water flows into a pond, this is not disguised, but made a deliberate part of the design. Everything around the inflow is edged with materials such as timber, rocks, or cobbles to keep it clean. Muddiness is not tolerated.

Should you want to incorporate a pond into your garden landscape, it should obviously be well positioned, but it must also look as though it's always been there.

Japanese ponds always have a focal point, normally a waterfall, but sometimes a bridge, island, or hill is used instead. This should always be at the far end of the pond from the viewer and must look to be inaccessible. You should not be able to view the entire pond from any single viewpoint.

The Japanese also design ponds to look irregular and natural, with the largest body of water closer to the viewpoint, diminishing the further away it gets. One traditional pond design is gourd shaped with a tree at one end and narrower in the middle to allow for a bridge.

Dry Water

Japanese garden designers used dry water and waterfalls for both practical and philosophical reasons. Dry landscapes represent the level of abstraction that was appealing to Zen. Real water was often costly and difficult to include in a design.

Water which is too pure has no fish.

If you're designing a dry landscape garden, you should do so as if water were actually present at the same time as respecting the basic principles of Japanese garden design. With dry water features, the need to simplify nature is more pronounced. For instance, a single stone set at ground level, carefully chosen, is all that will represent a waterfall.

Pebbles should be small, water-worn, and off-white or gray to suggest the reflective properties of water. They can be used to suggest upland rivers or streams. Adding the odd red or black pebble will create visual interest.

Instead of beach sand, you should use crushed granite or gravel which is usually off-white or gray, although it's sometimes flecked with brown or red specks. You can buy gravel like this from nurseries or stone merchants.

When you're raking a pattern into gravel, remember that the top level represents the water level. Around rocks you need to take care to make certain that the pattern looks convincing. Zen masters would meditate while raking.

Gravel reflects light, which adds to its appeal in courtyards. Both pebbles and gravel look superb when wet and the Japanese often spray them to bring out their beauty.

Dry waterfalls

The key element to a dry waterfall is the water-falling stone because it needs to suggest that water might start to flow at any moment. A water-falling stone should be vertical with a flat face at the front with an indentation at the top to show where the "water" flows.

Japanese designers particularly prize stones with striations down them because this is even more suggestive of falling water.

More Design Elements

The obstacle is the path.

Bridges

If the pond or stream you create is large enough to accommodate a bridge, it needs to work harmoniously with your garden design. You also need to think about consistency. For instance, if you've used a lot of stone you should try to make a one- or two-stone slab bridge.

Whatever style of bridge you choose, it's important that it should be able to take the weight of anyone wishing to try it. A bridge should both give support and be seen to be able to do so. As with any feature in a Japanese garden, a bridge cannot look false, and from a safety point of view it should be practically sound and function as a bridge.

54

Paths

Paths in Japanese gardens don't simply move people around a garden from place to place without them getting muddy. They're meant to direct movement around the garden, but the main purpose is to guide the mind and senses of the visitor.

Unlike in the West, some paths in Japanese gardens are never meant to be walked upon, apart from to provide access for garden maintenance. However, all paths serve a purpose.

Paths are a good way to use all the principles of perspective and composition favored by Japanese gardens. A straight path will take the eye along its length to the end, inviting the viewer to walk the path. The Japanese often place an important object like a beautiful water basin or the entrance to a temple at the end of such a path.

Curving paths take the eye on a journey. By following the curves, a new viewpoint and sensory experience can be revealed at every turn.

Both methods will lead people through the elements in a design. Using stepping-stone paths, which lead the eye toward an element, will make the visitor pause and contemplate.

You can exaggerate perspective by adjusting the width of a path: wider near a viewpoint and narrower as it heads off into the distance. Should you want to, you can also direct the viewers' movement—a broader area of path will cause them to linger and contemplate the feature of your choice.

Ornaments

A common mistake made by gardeners who become interested in Japanese garden design is to litter their garden with ornaments in the belief that it will look more authentic. Even though ornaments don't automatically make a garden Japanese, they can, if used carefully, enhance a design and become focal points.

Stone lanterns and water basins also have the practical function of enabling light and water to form part of your design.

Lanterns

There are a number of different styles of stone lantern. They were introduced into gardens by tea masters because tea ceremonies often took place in the evening and guests needed to be able to see where they were going.

56

If you do have a stone lantern, it will probably be for decorative purposes, but try to position it as if it were giving light. Place lanterns at path junctions, or near bridges or water basins.

When choosing a lantern, it's important to bear the scale of your garden design in mind.

Water basins

Like stone lanterns, water basins originated in ancient shrines and temples and were only later developed for use in the tea ceremony.

Genuine water basins are difficult to find in the West, so rather than buy an inferior water basin, it might be better, if less authentic, to use an urn.

Whether you're using a water basin or an urn, set it on the edge of a "sea" of water-worn cobbles in a shallow enclosure that can act as a drain.

Stupas and Buddhas

A stupa is a stone tower that can affect the perspective of a view, creating both a focal point and the illusion of distance. A good place for a stupa is by a stream or pond, where its reflection adds to the visual appeal.

Don't over-use stupas or Buddhas. A garden can only really accommodate one or two such pieces.

Miniature Zen Gardens

Highly detailed miniatures are now available and you can use a miniature Zen garden as an aid to relaxation and contemplation in your home or office.

According to Zen, as with feng shui, every part of our universe is worthy of respect and contemplation. This extends to your home or office life.

Large-scale Zen gardens can be an antidote to the stresses of modern living, but a miniature garden can also help you relax. They're easy to look after and won't clutter your living space.

Better to see
the face than
hear the name.

With a miniature Zen garden you reduce all the problems of your day—whether at home or at work—to the simple act of raking sand around rocks. You can lose yourself in patterns that are as intricate as you wish to create. This, in turn, will make you feel that your life has become simplified—that you are in control and less at the mercy of stress.

It will also make you more aware that you can just as easily contemplate the detail of life as you can its more spectacular manifestations.

Common raking patterns

Japanese dry gardens typically include these patterns. As you become more expert at raking your miniature garden, you can try the more complex patterns. More intricate designs can be made with other instruments, such as a cocktail stick or chopstick.

The empty corner

Using smooth, fluid movements, rake out ever decreasing corners until there are none left.

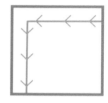

The arrows indicate the direction of rake movements.

The lone rock

To rake around a lone rock, try to systematically approach the rock from each of its sides. Follow the direction of the arrows using slow but firm strokes.

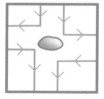

The pair of knights

Wiggle between two rocks by raking into the first rock and then turning into the second, following the direction of the arrows.

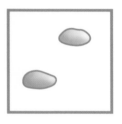 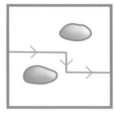 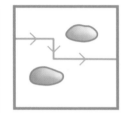

The loop

Use a chopstick or cocktail stick for more intricate patterns. This one comprises long, smooth strokes, with the pattern looping back on itself.

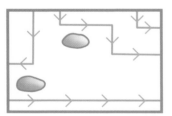 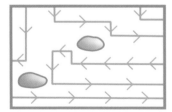

The kink

Rake toward the rock and then turn back on yourself with fluid movements.

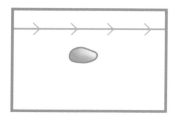
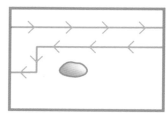

The circuit

Rake all the way around a rock in a systematic movement.

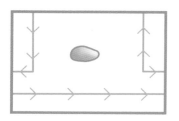
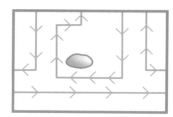

Zen Garden Meditations

Spring does not become summer. First there is spring, then summer. Each season stays in its proper place.

As more and more people are discovering, meditation is an excellent way of relaxing and handling the stresses of living in today's fast-moving world.

These are some simple meditation techniques that you can practice in your garden, at home, or even at work. You don't necessarily have to sit in an uncomfortable position or lie on the floor. The aim is to be comfortable enough to relax.

Mindfulness meditation

Buddhists say that this meditation was taught by the Buddha around 2,500 years ago. By focusing on your breathing, you aim to maintain a sense of calm, non-judgmental awareness.

The steps of mindfulness meditation

According to Buddhists, when you've reached a state of calm, accepting awareness, you've arrived at your core self or essence. Try to meditate for at least twenty minutes, building up the amount of time gradually.

- Sit comfortably with your eyes closed and your spine reasonably straight.

- Focus on relaxed, measured breathing.

- If thoughts, emotions, physical sensations, or sounds arise, acknowledge and accept them and let them pass without becoming involved.

- When you notice your attention has become caught up on a thought, emotion, or sensation, focus on your breathing again before carrying on.

The benefits

- You learn to maintain your calm, inner awareness and a sense of clarity, whatever the situation.

- There is a shift to a higher level of consciousness where you discover a sense of peace, joy, and freedom.

- Your stress levels will be reduced.

Conclusion

Both Zen and Japanese garden designs are rich, mysterious, and fascinating subjects that people spend their lives studying and creating.

The beauty of even the briefest introduction to either lies in the fact that it can change the way you look at your life, sometimes in an instant.

A simple Buddhist meditation might hold the key to enabling you to relax at home or work, even for a couple of minutes. Reading a Zen Buddhist koan might help you gain a perspective on challenges facing you in your own life.

Whether you are a keen gardener or not, it's impossible not to find Japanese Zen gardens both beautiful and intriguing. You might be inspired to create your own garden and one of the great things about Japanese gardens is that they can be created in even the smallest of spaces.

Look to this day,
for it is life.
In its brief course
lies all the
realities of
our existence.

Acknowledgments
Key: Top - t; middle - m;
bottom - b; left - l; right - r;
Front Cover: iStock
9: imagemore.
11: Topham Picture Point.
18: Betty Mallorca/Corbis.
31: Rex Butcher/Garden Picture Library.
1 & 33: Catherine Karnow/Corbis.
42 & 44: Courtesy of The Bonsai Nursery.
50: Rex Features.
52: Charles+Josette Lenars/Corbis.
55: Joel Katz/Corbis.
56: Benjamin Rondel/Corbis.
59-61: TT.
All other images by Corel.